The Power of Silence
30 Day Course Book
Daily Transformative Activities

Biography of Silence, Solitude & Stillness Meditation.
Supporting Mental Health, Anxiety, Decision Making,
Anger Management, Health, Wealth, Relationships

Guided Transformations

Copyright © 2024

All rights reserved. Without limiting rights under the copyright reserved above, no part of this publication may be reproduced, stored, introduced into a retrieval system, distributed or transmitted in any form or by any means, including without limitation photocopying, recording, or other electronic or mechanical methods, without the prior written permission of the publisher, except in the case of brief quotations embodied in critical reviews and certain other non-commercial uses permitted by copyright law.

This book, with the opinions, suggestions and references made within it, is based on the author's personal experience and is for personal study and research purposes only. This program is about health and vitality, not disease. The author makes no medical claims. If you choose to use the material in this book on yourself, the author and publisher take no responsibility for your actions and decisions or the consequences thereof..

The scanning, uploading, and/or distribution of this document via the internet or via any other means without the permission of the publisher is illegal and is punishable by law. Please purchase only authorized editions and do not participate in or encourage electronic piracy of copyrightable materials

Introduction

Welcome to this 30-day silence workbook, which we have created to help you implement practices to improve your personal development, daily performance, and mental and physical health.

When harnessed correctly, silence can have a profound impact on our lives. Over the next 30 days, with the daily exercises, we'll dive deep into the tranquillity and inner peace that silence offers, uncovering its many benefits for our physical, emotional, and spiritual well-being.

In today's fast-paced life, the art of silence is often drowned out in the noise. We're bombarded by distractions, from the buzz of various social media platforms to the hum of everyday life. Amidst this chaos, the power of silence can slip through our fingers, leaving us feeling disconnected and overwhelmed. It's not just you, this is a common struggle in our modern world.

But what if we could reclaim silence and use it to find clarity and calm? What if we could listen to the whispers of our hearts and souls amidst the stillness? What if we could lower the volume on any negative inner talk, such as self-doubt or self-criticism, or limiting beliefs that hinder our progress, such as 'I'm not good enough' or 'I can't do it '? That's exactly what this workbook is about – a journey to rediscover the immense power of silence and its potential to take you to the next level.

Over the next 30 days, we'll engage in activities designed to deepen our connection with silence. From mindful breathing to moments of quiet contemplation, each day offers a new opportunity to embrace the power of stillness and find peace within.

As you work your way through each day's activity, we invite you to approach it with an open mind and a willingness to explore. Let yourself be guided by the wisdom of silence, trusting that it holds the key to unlocking your true self. Rest assured, each activity is designed to support your journey and provide you with the necessary guidance.

We are embarking on a transformative journey that will delve into the depths of stillness, unlocking the wisdom of silence by helping you cultivate a deeper sense of self-awareness and inner peace. Along the way, we'll also discover beauty in life's quiet moments, learning to appreciate the simple joys and finding inspiration in the silence.

This journey is about empowering you with tools for personal growth that you can use whenever you need them.

Let's begin!

Day 1:

Introduction to Silence

Activity Summary: Take 10 minutes to sit in a quiet space and reflect on what silence means to you personally. Consider how silence can benefit your mind, body, and soul.

Day 1 Activity: Reflective Silence Session

Instructions:

1. Find a comfortable and quiet space where you can sit for the next 10 minutes without interruptions. You could sit in a cosy area in your home, a serene spot in nature, or any place where you feel at ease and free from distractions.

2. Sit in a relaxed yet alert posture, allowing your body to settle comfortably. You may sit on a cushion or chair with your back straight and your hands resting gently on your lap. Close your eyes or soften your gaze, whichever feels most natural.

3. Take a few deep breaths to centre yourself and bring your awareness into the present moment. Feel the sensation of your breath as it flows in and out of your body, grounding you in the here and now.

4. Begin your reflective silence session by contemplating the meaning of silence in your life. What does silence represent to you? How do you currently experience silence, if at all? Take a few moments to explore these questions with an open mind and heart.

5. Consider the potential benefits of incorporating silence into your daily routine. How might silence contribute to your mental, physical, and spiritual well-being? Reflect on past experiences where silence has played a positive role in your life or offered moments of clarity and insight.

6. Allow yourself to fully immerse in the stillness and quiet of the present moment. Notice any sounds or sensations around you without judgement or attachment. Observe and

acknowledge whatever arises in your awareness, allowing it to come and go like passing clouds in the sky.

7. Use this time to connect with your inner self and listen to the whispers of your heart and soul. Tune into your intuition and inner wisdom, trusting that they will guide you on your journey of self-discovery and personal growth.

8. As you conclude your reflective silence session, take a few moments to express gratitude for this opportunity to connect with silence and yourself. Offer thanks for the insights gained and the potential for growth that lies ahead.

Real-Life Examples

a) James sits by the window in his favourite armchair, gazing at the tranquil garden bathed in soft morning light. As he closes his eyes and takes a deep breath, he reflects on the stillness around him and the sense of calm it evokes. He realises that silence offers him a sanctuary for introspection and self-reflection, allowing him to reconnect with his innermost thoughts and feelings.

b) Maya strolls along the forest trail near her home, surrounded by the gentle rustle of leaves and the melodic chirping of birds. She embraces the peace and serenity of nature's symphony as she finds a quiet clearing to sit and reflect. She recognises that silence in nature provides her with a profound sense of harmony and connection, nurturing her soul and replenishing her spirit.

c) David sets aside time each evening to unwind and decompress in his cosy meditation corner. As he settles into his meditation cushion and closes his eyes, he welcomes the soothing silence that envelops him like a warm embrace. He acknowledges that silence serves as a refuge from the chaos of daily life, offering him a sanctuary where he can find solace and inner peace.

Embrace this opportunity to explore the depths of silence and discover its transformative power in your life. Allow yourself to cultivate a deeper appreciation for its beauty and richness, and let it become a source of inspiration and renewal on your journey toward greater well-being and fulfilment.

Day 2:

Understanding the Physical Benefits of Silence

Activity Summary: Practise deep breathing exercises for 15 minutes to experience the physical relaxation that silence can bring.

Day 2 Activity: Exploring the Physical Benefits of Silence: Engage in Mindful Breathing for Physical Relaxation

Instructions:

1. Set aside 15 minutes in a quiet, comfortable space where you won't be disturbed.

2. Find a comfortable seated position (on a chair or a cushion) with your back straightened and your hands resting on your lap or knees.

3. Close your eyes gently or maintain a soft gaze, whichever feels most comfortable.

4. Begin to focus on your breath, noticing the sensation of each inhale and exhale as they enter and leave your body.

5. Take slow, deep breaths, allowing your abdomen to inflate and deflate with each inhalation and exhalation.

6. Pay attention to the rhythm of your breath, letting it guide you into a state of relaxation and calm.

7. If your mind wanders, calmly bring your attention back to your breathing without judgement or frustration.

8. Continue this mindful breathing practice for the entire 15 minutes of the exercise, allowing yourself to fully experience the physical relaxation that comes with silence and focused breathing.

Real-Life Examples

a) Sarah sets aside 15 minutes during her lunch break to practise mindful breathing in her office. She closes the door, dims the lights, and sits comfortably in her chair, taking slow, deep breaths as she focuses on the sensation of air entering and leaving her body. With each breath, she feels tension melting away from her muscles, leaving her feeling refreshed and rejuvenated for the rest of her day.

b) Before starting work, Alex incorporates mindful breathing into his morning routine. He finds a quiet spot in his living room, sits cross-legged on a cushion and closes his eyes as he begins to breathe deeply and intentionally. As he continues the practice, he notices his mind becoming clearer and his body feeling more relaxed, setting a positive tone for the day ahead.

c) Emily practises mindful breathing before bedtime to help her unwind and prepare for sleep. She lies down on her back in bed, closes her eyes, and focuses on her breath as she inhales and exhales deeply. With each breath, she feels her body sinking deeper into the mattress, allowing her to drift off into a peaceful and restful sleep.

Day 3:

Exploring the Spiritual Aspects of Silence

Activity Summary: Embark on a 20-minute personal journey of silent contemplation, where you focus on connecting with your inner self and exploring your unique spiritual essence.

Day 3 Activity: Delving into the Spiritual Dimensions of Silence: Engage in 20 Minutes of Silent Contemplation for Spiritual Connection. Remember, your spiritual journey is unique to you, and this activity is designed to support your personal exploration.

Instructions:

1. Find a safe and comfortable space, free from distractions, where you can sit up for 20 minutes. This is your sanctuary for the practice.

2. Close your eyes gently or maintain a soft gaze, whichever feels most comfortable. Remember that you don't want to fall asleep during this exercise, as the goal is to maintain a state of relaxed alertness, not to enter a sleep state.

3. Breathe in and breathe out as you become centred and bring your awareness to the present moment.

4. Begin by directing your attention inward, focusing on the sensations in your body and the rhythm of your breath.

5. Allow thoughts or emotions to pass through your awareness without judgement or attachment simply.

6. Shift your focus to exploring your spiritual essence, which refers to the core of your being, your true self beyond the physical body and thoughts. Ask yourself questions such as 'Who am I beyond my physical body and thoughts?' or 'What brings meaning and purpose to my life?'

7. Notice any insights, intuitions, or feelings of connection that arise during your silent contemplation, allowing

them to inspire and guide you deeper into your spiritual exploration.

8. Embrace the profound silence as a sacred space, a place where you can commune with your inner self and the divine. Trust in the wisdom and guidance that arises from within during this sacred time.

Real-Life Examples

a) Mark finds a quiet corner in his home where he can sit comfortably on a cushion. He closes his eyes and begins his silent contemplation by focusing on his breath. As he delves deeper into his inner world, he feels a sense of peace and clarity wash over him, allowing him to connect with a profound sense of spiritual presence within himself.

b) Rachel takes a walk in nature, allowing the beauty and serenity of her surroundings to inspire her silent contemplation. She finds a peaceful spot by a tranquil stream and sits quietly, absorbing the sights and sounds of the natural world around her. In the stillness of the forest, she feels a deep sense of connection with something greater than herself, nurturing her spirit and replenishing her soul.

c) Sarah lights a candle and creates a sacred space in her home for her silent contemplation practice. She sits before the flickering flame, allowing its gentle light to illuminate her inner world. As she closes her eyes and turns her attention inward, she feels a profound sense of peace and inner knowing wash over her, reminding her of the infinite wisdom and guidance within her soul.

Day 4:

Implementing Silence in Daily Life

Activity Summary: Designate one hour of your day to be completely silent. Turn off all electronic devices and embrace the stillness around you.

Day 4 Activity: Silent Hour

Instructions:

1. Choose a one-hour time slot in your day when you can commit to being completely silent - this could be in the morning, afternoon, or evening, depending on your schedule and preferences.

2. Before your silent hour begins, inform anyone you live with or interact with regularly about your intention to observe silence during this time, letting them know that you won't be engaging in conversation or communication. Ask for their support and understanding.

3. Turn off all electronic devices, including your phone, computer, television, and any other sources of noise or distraction. Dim the lights, close curtains or blinds, and minimise external stimuli to create a peaceful environment.

4. Find a comfortable space to sit up without interruptions - this could be your living room, bedroom, or even outdoors in nature if the weather permits. Ensure you have everything within reach so you won't need to break your silence.

5. Begin your silent hour by taking a few deep breaths to centre yourself and quiet your mind. Allow yourself to relax into the stillness and embrace the present moment without needing words or external stimulation.

6. Use this time to engage in quiet activities that nourish your mind, body, and soul. You could read a book, practise gentle yoga or meditation, take a leisurely walk in nature, or sit in contemplative silence, observing your thoughts and feelings as they arise.

7. If your mind starts to wander or you feel tempted to break your silence, gently redirect your focus to the present moment. Use your breath as an anchor to guide you back to inner calm and serenity.

8. As your silent hour ends, reflect on your experience briefly. Notice any changes in your mood, energy levels, or mental clarity that may have occurred due to observing silence. Consider how you can incorporate more moments of calm into your daily life moving forward.

Real-Life Examples

a) James sets aside the hour before bedtime as his designated silent hour. He turns off his phone, dims the lights in his bedroom, and settles into his favourite armchair with a book. As he reads in silence, he feels a sense of peace and relaxation wash over him, allowing him to unwind from the day's stresses and prepare for a restful night's sleep.

b) Maria decides to observe her silent hour during her lunch break at work. She finds a quiet spot in the park near her office, away from the hustle and bustle of the city streets. Sitting on a bench surrounded by nature, Maria takes deep breaths of fresh air and listens to birds chirping and leaves rustling in the breeze. In the moment's stillness, she feels a profound connection to the world around her and a renewed appreciation for the beauty of life.

c) David chooses to spend his silent hour in the early morning before the rest of his family wakes up. He tiptoes downstairs to the living room, where he sits in front of the window overlooking his garden. As David gazes at the peaceful scene outside, he sips a cup of herbal tea and reflects on his intentions for the day ahead. In the quiet solitude of the morning, he feels inspired and invigorated, ready to tackle whatever challenges come his way with grace and resilience.

Take this opportunity to implement silence into your daily life by observing a silent hour. Embrace the stillness around you and allow yourself to connect more deeply with your inner self and the world around you.

Day 5:

Retreat to Nature

Activity Summary: Take a 30-minute walk in nature. Listen to the sounds of the natural world and connect with the silence beneath the noise.

Day 5 Activity: Nature Walk

Instructions:

1. Find a nearby natural setting where you can walk for about 30 minutes - a local park, nature reserve, forest trail, beach, or any outdoor environment that appeals to you.

2. Before you walk, take a few moments to prepare yourself mentally. Leave behind any distractions or worries from your daily life and enter this natural space with an open mind and heart.

3. As you start walking, pay close attention to your surroundings. Notice the sights, sounds, smells, and sensations of the natural world around you. Take deep breaths of fresh air and fully immerse yourself in nature's beauty.

4. Tune in to the sounds of the environment. Listen to the birds singing, the leaves rustling in the wind, the gentle flow of water in a nearby stream, or any other natural sounds you encounter. Allow these sounds to wash over you and bring peace and tranquillity to your mind and body.

5. As you walk, be mindful of your footsteps and the rhythm of your breath. Let go of any racing thoughts or mental chatter and focus on being fully present in the moment. Feel the earth beneath your feet and the connection between yourself and the natural world.

6. Explore the natural surroundings at a leisurely pace. Pause occasionally to admire the beauty of a flower, the intricate patterns of tree bark, or the play of light and shadow through the branches. Allow yourself to be captivated by

the wonders of nature and the silent symphony that unfolds all around you.

7. As you walk, reflect on the silence beneath the noise. Consider how nature embodies this idea, with its serene stillness underlying the vibrant tapestry of life. Reflect on how you can cultivate this inner silence within yourself, even amidst the busyness of daily life.

8. After about 30 minutes of walking, find a quiet spot to sit and rest briefly. Close your eyes and take a few deep breaths, allowing yourself to bask in the peace and serenity of the natural environment. Take this time to express gratitude for retreating to nature and connecting with the silence within.

Real-Life Examples

a) Sarah decides to take her nature walk in a nearby botanical garden. As she strolls along the winding pathways, she listens to the soothing sounds of water trickling from a fountain and the chirping of birds hidden among the trees. Sarah takes her time to appreciate the vibrant colours of the flowers and the refreshing scent of the greenery around her. With each step, she feels more grounded and connected to the natural world, finding solace in the quiet moments of reflection.

b) Mark chooses to explore a nearby forest trail for his nature walk. As he hikes through the dense woods, he listens to the rustling of leaves underfoot and the distant call of a woodpecker echoing through the trees. Mark takes his time to admire the towering pines and the dappled sunlight filtering through the canopy above. With each breath of fresh forest air, he feels a sense of calm and clarity wash over him, allowing him to let go of the stresses of everyday life and find peace in the present moment.

c) Emily opts to visit a local beach for her nature walk. As she walks along the sandy shore, she listens to the rhythmic crashing of waves against the shore and the cries of seagulls soaring overhead. Emily watches the sunlight dance on the water's surface and feels the cool breeze caress her skin. With each step, she feels more connected to the ocean's vast expanse and the natural world's timeless beauty, finding serenity in the simplicity of the moment.

Take this opportunity to retreat to nature and experience the profound connection between silence and the natural world. Immerse yourself in the sights, sounds, and sensations of nature as you embark on a refreshing nature walk.

Day 6:

Deep Listening

Activity Summary: Practise active listening during conversations today. Focus on genuinely hearing what others say without interrupting or formulating your response.

Day 6 Activity: Practise Active Listening

Instructions:

1. Throughout the day, make a conscious effort to listen during your conversations with others actively. Whether you're speaking with family members, friends, colleagues, or strangers, strive to hear and understand what they're saying honestly.

2. Begin each conversation by listening attentively. Set aside distractions like electronic devices or wandering thoughts, and give the speaker your full attention.

3. As the other person speaks, focus on their words without interrupting or formulating your response. Instead of thinking about what you'll say next, absorb their message and understand their perspective.

4. Pay attention not only to the words spoken but also to the speaker's tone of voice, body language, and emotional cues. These nonverbal signals can provide valuable insights into the speaker's thoughts and feelings.

5. Practice empathy and compassion as you listen. Try to put yourself in the speaker's shoes and imagine how they might be experiencing the situation. Show genuine interest in their thoughts and feelings, and validate their experiences by acknowledging their emotions.

6. Use active listening techniques, such as paraphrasing or summarising the speaker's words, to demonstrate that you're actively engaged in the conversation. Reflect on their words to ensure you've understood them correctly and convey your respect for their perspective.

7. Resist the urge to rush or interrupt the speaker, even if you have thoughts or opinions to share. Remember that active listening gives the speaker space to express themselves fully and feel heard and understood.

8. After the conversation, take a moment to reflect on your experience of practising deep listening. Consider how it felt to truly engage with the speaker and how it impacted your connection with them. Notice any insights or revelations that arose from the experience.

Real-Life Examples

a) Sarah actively listens during a conversation with her co-worker about a challenging project at work. Instead of immediately offering solutions or advice, she listens attentively as her co-worker shares their concerns and ideas. Sarah nods encouragingly and asks clarifying questions to ensure she understands the situation entirely. By the end of the conversation, her co-worker expresses gratitude for her support and feels heard and validated.

b) Mark practises deep listening during a discussion with his wife about their weekend plans. Instead of zoning out or multitasking, he maintains eye contact. He gives his wife undivided attention while listening to her attentively as they share their preferences and desires, trying to empathise with their perspective. As a result, they can come to a mutually satisfying agreement that honours both of their needs.

c) Emily practises active listening during a conversation with her friend who is going through a difficult time. Instead of trying to cheer her up or offer advice, Emily listens with an open heart, allowing her friend to express her emotions freely. She nods in understanding and gives words of empathy and support, validating her friend's feelings and providing a safe space for her to process her emotions.

By practising active listening, you can deepen your connections with others, foster mutual understanding, and cultivate empathy and compassion in your relationships. Take this opportunity to hone your listening skills and experience the transformative power of deep listening in your interactions with others.

Day 7:

Silent Meditation

Activity Summary: Dedicate 20 minutes to silent meditation. Find a comfortable position, close your eyes, and focus on your breath or a mantra.

Day 7 Activity: Dedicate 20 Minutes to Silent Meditation

Instructions:

1. Find a quiet and comfortable space where you won't be disturbed for 20 minutes, including a peaceful corner of your home, a tranquil outdoor setting, or any place where you feel relaxed and at ease.

2. Sit down comfortably, ensuring your spine is straight and your body is well-supported. You can achieve this by sitting on a cushion or a chair with a straight back. Close your eyes gently and take a few deep breaths to centre yourself and prepare for meditation.

3. Begin by bringing your awareness to your breath. Notice the sensation of the air flowing in and out of your nostrils, the rise and fall of your chest or abdomen with each breath, and the rhythm of your breathing. Allow your breath to guide you into relaxation and inner stillness. Inner stillness refers to a state of calm and quiet within your mind and body, where you are fully present and free from distractions.

4. As you focus on your breath, let go of any tension or stress you may be holding in your body and mind. If you experience any physical discomfort, such as aching muscles or a restless leg, try adjusting your posture or gently stretching to alleviate the discomfort. Allow yourself to release any thoughts or distractions that arise, gently returning your attention to your breath whenever your mind wanders.

5. If you find it helpful, you can also choose a mantra or a word to focus on during your meditation. For example, you could use 'peace ', 'calm ', or 'love '. Repeat this word silently to yourself with each inhalation and exhalation, allowing it to anchor your mind and deepen your meditation practice.

6. As you remain in silent meditation, allow yourself to be in the present moment, fully accepting whatever arises without judgement or resistance. Embrace the silence and stillness within you, allowing it to nourish your body, mind, and soul.

7. If your mind becomes restless or distracted during the meditation, gently guide your focus back to your breath or mantra, using it as a point of concentration to anchor yourself in the present moment. If you find yourself falling asleep, try opening your eyes slightly or adjusting your posture to stay alert.

8. Continue to meditate silently for the next 20 minutes, allowing yourself to experience a deep sense of peace, tranquillity, and inner calm. Please note that maintaining focus during silent meditation can be challenging, especially for beginners. However, with practice, it becomes easier. Trust in the power of silence to quiet the mind, open the heart, and connect you to the essence of your being.

Real-Life Examples

a) Sarah begins her silent meditation practice by finding a cosy spot in her living room to sit comfortably on a cushion with her back against the wall. She closes her eyes gently and takes deep breaths to relax her body and mind. As Sarah settles into the meditation, she focuses on her breathing, allowing its rhythmic pattern to soothe her nerves and quiet her thoughts. With each inhalation and exhalation, she feels herself sinking deeper into a state of peaceful awareness, letting go of any tension or stress she may have been carrying.

b) Mark meditates outdoors in his back garden, surrounded by the soothing sounds of nature and the sun's warmth on his skin. He finds a comfortable spot on a blanket beneath a shady tree where he can lie down and fully relax. Closing his eyes, Mark focuses on his breath, feeling his chest's gentle rise and fall with each inhalation and exhalation. As he breathes deeply, he feels a sense of connection to the natural world around him, allowing his environment's sights, sounds, and sensations to deepen his meditation practice.

c) Emily opts for a silent meditation practice in her bedroom, where she can sit quietly on a cushion at the foot of her bed. With her eyes closed and her hands resting gently on her knees, she silently repeats a calming mantra to herself with each breath. As Emily meditates, she feels a sense of inner peace and clarity wash over her, releasing any worries or concerns she may have been holding onto. In the silence of her meditation, she discovers a profound sense of stillness and serenity, allowing her to connect more deeply with her innermost self.

By dedicating time to silent meditation, you can cultivate a sense of inner peace, clarity, and presence in your life. Silent meditation allows you to quiet the mind, reduce stress, and enhance self-awareness. Take this opportunity to immerse yourself in the practice of meditation and experience the transformative power of silence on your journey of self-discovery and spiritual growth.

Day 8:

Silence in Creativity

Activity Summary: Engage in a creative activity without any background noise. Allow silence to inspire your creativity, Whether drawing, writing, or crafting.

Day 8 Activity: Engage in a Creative Activity Without Background Noise

Instructions:

1. Choose a creative activity that you enjoy and feel passionate about. Some examples include drawing, painting, writing, crafting, playing a musical instrument, or any other creative expression that speaks to you.

2. Find a quiet, comfortable workplace space without distractions or background noise. This could be a peaceful corner of your home, a serene outdoor setting, or any place you feel inspired and focused.

3. Gather all the necessary materials and tools for your chosen creative activity. Whether it's a blank canvas and paints, a notebook and pen, or a set of knitting needles and yarn, ensure you have everything you need to bring your creative vision to life.

4. Once ready, take a few deep breaths to centre yourself and quiet your mind. Close your eyes briefly and visualise the creative process unfolding effortlessly before you. Imagine yourself fully immersed in the flow of inspiration, letting your intuition guide your hands and thoughts.

5. Begin your creative activity in silence, allowing the absence of background noise to enhance your focus and concentration. Pay attention to the subtle sounds of your materials and tools as you work, the brush strokes on canvas, the scratch of pencil on paper, or the rhythmic clicking of knitting needles.

6. Embrace the silence as a source of inspiration and creativity, allowing it to guide your thoughts and ideas without external distractions. Trust your innate creative instincts and let your imagination free as you explore new possibilities and express yourself authentically.

7. If you find your mind wandering or struggling to stay focused, gently bring your attention back to the present moment and the creative task. Take a moment to re-centre yourself with a few deep breaths, grounding yourself in the silence and stillness of the present.

8. Allow yourself to fully immerse in the creative process, losing track of time and surrendering to the flow of inspiration. Let go of any expectations or judgments, allowing your creativity to unfold organically and authentically in the silence.

Real-Life Examples

a) Sarah, an aspiring artist, decides to spend her day painting in the quiet solitude of her backyard. Armed with her canvas, brushes, and acrylic paints, she sets up her easel beneath a shady tree and begins to sketch out her vision. As Sarah dips her brush into the vibrant colours and sweeps them across the canvas, she loses herself in the creative flow, letting the silence around her amplify her focus and inspiration. With each brushstroke, she feels a sense of freedom and expression, allowing her artistic vision to come to life in the tranquil embrace of silence.

b) Mark, a budding writer, retreats to his favourite spot in the local library to work on his novel without distractions. Armed with his notebook and pen, he settles into a cosy corner surrounded by towering bookshelves and the soft murmur of turning pages. As Mark begins to write, he immerses himself in the world of his characters, letting the library's silence fuel his creativity and imagination. With each word he writes, he feels a sense of clarity and purpose, allowing his story to unfold organically and authentically in the peaceful ambience of the library.

c) a passionate crafter, Emily spends her afternoon knitting in the peaceful tranquillity of her living room. With her knitting needles clacking softly and the yarn slipping through her fingers, she loses herself in the rhythmic motion of her craft. As Emily stitches and purls, she feels a sense of calm and contentment wash over her, allowing the silence to amplify her creativity and focus. With each row she completes, she feels a sense of accomplishment and satisfaction, knowing that she has embraced the power of silence to inspire her creative expression.

By engaging in a creative activity without background noise, you can tap into the transformative power of silence to enhance your focus, concentration, and inspiration. Take this opportunity to immerse yourself fully in the creative process and let the silence guide your artistic expression in new and meaningful ways.

Day 9:

Embracing Solitude

Activity Summary: Spend 1 hour alone in complete silence. Use this time for introspection, journaling, or simply being present with your thoughts.

Day 9 Activity: Spend 1 Hour Alone in Complete Silence

Instructions:

1. Find a private and comfortable space for the next hour. This could be a cosy corner in your home, a secluded natural spot, or any place where you feel safe and at peace.

2. Set aside all distractions, including electronic devices, books, and other forms of entertainment. Create a space free from external stimuli to immerse yourself fully in silence and solitude.

3. Sit up comfortably, allowing yourself to settle into the present moment. Close your eyes if it feels comfortable, and take a few deep breaths to centre yourself and quiet your mind.

4. Use this time for introspection and self-reflection. Allow your thoughts and emotions to surface without judgement, observing them with curiosity and compassion. Reflect on your experiences, desires, and aspirations, exploring the depths of your inner world.

5. If you feel called to do so, consider journaling about your thoughts and feelings during this time of solitude. Write freely and openly, allowing your words to flow without censorship or restraint. Use your journal for self-discovery and personal growth, capturing insights and revelations from the silence within.

6. Alternatively, you may be present with your thoughts, allowing them to come and go like clouds passing through the sky. Practice mindfulness and awareness, tuning into

the sensations of your body and the rhythm of your breath. Allow yourself to experience the present moment fully without attachment or aversion.

7. Embrace the solitude as an opportunity for self-care and nourishment. Use this time to recharge and replenish your energy reserves, nurturing yourself on a deep level. Trust in the power of silence to soothe your soul and replenish your spirit, allowing yourself to bask in the peaceful embrace of solitude.

8. As the hour ends, take a moment to express gratitude for this precious gift of silence and solitude. Acknowledge the insights and revelations you've gained during this time, and carry them with you as you return to the world refreshed and renewed.

Real-Life Examples

a) a busy professional, Rachel decides to spend her hour of solitude in her backyard garden. Surrounded by the beauty of nature, she sits on a bench beneath a blossoming cherry tree, allowing herself to be captured by the sights and sounds of the natural world. As Rachel closes her eyes and takes a deep breath, she feels a sense of peace and tranquillity wash over her, allowing her to connect with her innermost thoughts and emotions. With each passing moment, she feels a profound sense of gratitude for this sacred time of solitude, knowing that it offers her the opportunity to recharge and replenish her spirit.

b) David, a college student, spends his hour of solitude in his dorm room. He turns off his phone and computer, disconnecting from the outside world and creating a space without distractions. Sitting cross-legged on his bed, David takes deep breaths to centre himself and quiet his mind. As he reflects on his experiences and goals, he feels a sense of clarity and purpose emerge. With each passing minute, he feels more deeply connected to himself and the world around him, knowing that this time of solitude allows him to explore his innermost thoughts and feelings in a safe and nurturing environment.

c) Maria, a stay-at-home mom, opts to spend her hour of solitude in her favourite cosy corner of the house. She brews herself a cup of herbal tea and settles into her favourite armchair, surrounded by pillows and blankets. As Maria sips her tea and gazes out the window at the changing colours of the sunset, she feels a sense of serenity and contentment wash over her. With each passing moment, she feels more deeply connected to herself and the world around her, knowing that this time of solitude offers her the opportunity to recharge and replenish her spirit after a long day of caring for her family.

Embracing solitude and time alone can cultivate a more profound self-awareness, inner peace, and emotional well-being. Use this time to reconnect with yourself profoundly, allowing the silence to nourish your soul and replenish your spirit.

Day 10:

Reflecting on Past Silence

Activity Summary: Journal about your experiences with silence so far and reflect on any insights or discoveries you've made.

Day 10 Activity: Journal About Your Experiences with Silence So Far

Instructions:

1. Set aside some quiet time and find a comfortable space to reflect and write without interruption. This could be a cosy corner in your home, a peaceful natural spot, or anywhere else where you feel relaxed and at ease.

2. Take out your journal or a blank piece of paper and a pen, and prepare to engage in a reflective writing exercise. Review your silence experiences over the past ten days, recalling any moments of stillness, contemplation, or solitude that stand out to you.

3. Reflect on the various activities you've engaged in, from silent meditation to deep breathing exercises to spending time alone in nature. Consider how these practices have impacted your mind, body, and spirit and what insights or discoveries you've made.

4. Write freely and openly about your experiences, thoughts, and emotions. Use your journal as a safe and sacred space to explore the depths of your inner world, allowing your words to flow without judgement or restraint. Be honest and authentic in your reflections, expressing yourself in whatever feels most natural.

5. Consider any challenges or obstacles you've encountered during your journey with silence and how you've overcome them or grown from them. Reflect on the lessons and wisdom you've gained through your experiences, acknowledging the value of both the highs and the lows.

6. Explore how your relationship with silence has evolved over the past ten days and how it has influenced other areas of your life. Notice any changes in your mindset, behaviour, or outlook and how these changes have impacted your overall well-being and sense of fulfilment.

7. Express gratitude for the gift of silence and the opportunity to deepen your understanding of yourself and the world around you. Acknowledge the transformative power of silence in your life, and commit to continuing your journey of exploration and self-discovery in the days and weeks to come.

Real-Life Examples

a) Sarah sits down with her journal and reflects on her experiences with silence over the past week. She recalls the sense of calm and clarity she felt during her silent walks in nature, as well as the profound insights that arose during her moments of meditation. Sarah writes about her challenges in quieting her busy mind and her strategies to overcome them, such as focusing on her breath or repeating a calming mantra. As she delves deeper into her reflections, she realises how much she has learned about herself and the importance of carving out moments of stillness in her daily life.

b) James takes time to journal his journey with silence so far. He reflects on the sense of peace and serenity he experienced during his hour of solitude and the powerful emotions that surfaced during his silent meditation sessions. James writes about the insights he gained into his own thoughts and feelings and the renewed sense of purpose and clarity he feels about his goals and aspirations. As he pours his thoughts onto the page, he feels a profound gratitude for the opportunity to explore the depths of his inner world and connect with the wisdom of silence.

c) Maya opens her journal and begins to reflect on her experiences with silence over the past week. She writes about the challenges she faced in quieting her mind and the moments of frustration and doubt that arose along the way. Maya also writes about the moments of joy and peace she experienced when she fully embraced the silence and connected with her inner self. Reflecting on her journey, she realises how much she has grown and learned in just a short period, and she feels a deep sense of gratitude for the transformative power of silence in her life.

Reflecting on your experiences with silence so far can give you valuable insights into yourself and your relationship with the world around you. Use this journaling activity to deepen your understanding of the benefits of silence and reaffirm your commitment to embracing stillness in your daily life.

Day 11:

Silence in Communication

Activity Summary: Practise mindful communication today. Listen attentively to others and choose your words thoughtfully, embracing moments of silence when necessary.

Day 11 Activity: Practise Mindful Communication Today

Instructions:

1. Begin your day with a conscious intention to practise mindful communication in all your interactions. Whether you're speaking with family members, friends, colleagues, or strangers, strive to listen attentively and choose your words thoughtfully throughout the day.

2. As you engage in conversations, focus on being fully present and attentive to the speaker. Avoid the temptation to multitask or mentally prepare your response while they're talking. Instead, please give them your undivided attention, maintaining eye contact and nodding or offering verbal cues to indicate that you're actively listening.

3. Practise active listening, a key component of mindful communication. This involves paraphrasing or summarising what the speaker has said to ensure accurate understanding. Use reflective listening techniques, such as repeating back key points or asking clarifying questions, to demonstrate your genuine interest and empathy. Active listening is not just about hearing the words but about understanding the message and the emotions behind it.

4. Be mindful of your speech patterns and communication style. Pause and consider your words before speaking, especially in situations where emotions may be running high or sensitive topics are being discussed. Choose transparent, respectful, and considerate language of the other person's feelings and perspectives.

5. Embrace moments of silence during conversations, recognizing its power in fostering deeper understanding and connection. Silence can be a valuable tool, allowing both parties to process information and formulate thoughtful responses. It's not just the absence of words, but a space for reflection and contemplation that can significantly enhance your communication experience.

Pay close attention to nonverbal cues, such as facial expressions, body language, and tone of voice, to gain deeper insight into the speaker's emotions and intentions. This practice of empathy and compassion in your interactions is crucial for fostering understanding and connection. Seek to understand the underlying emotions and needs behind their words, and you'll find yourself feeling more connected and compassionate towards others.

At the end of the day, take a moment to reflect on your experiences with mindful communication. Consider how your intentional focus on listening and thoughtful speech has impacted the quality of your interactions and relationships. Notice any shifts in your communication habits or awareness of the power of silence in fostering deeper connections with others. This self-reflection is a powerful tool for personal growth, empowering you to take control of your communication skills and improve them further.

Real-Life Examples

a) Sarah begins her day with a commitment to practising mindful communication in her interactions. During a team meeting at work, she listens attentively to her colleagues' ideas and contributions, refraining from interrupting or rushing to share her thoughts. When it's her turn to speak, Sarah takes a moment to pause and consider her words carefully, ensuring that they convey respect and appreciation for her coworkers' perspectives. She embraces moments of silence during conversations throughout the day, allowing space for reflection and mutual understanding.

b) James strives to practise mindful communication as he interacts with his family members at home. During dinner discussions, he listens actively to his children's stories and experiences, offering his full attention and support. When his partner shares their thoughts and concerns, he responds thoughtfully, choosing his words with care and compassion. James also recognizes the importance of nonverbal communication, using gestures and expressions to convey empathy and understanding. Embracing moments of silence during conversations creates space for deeper connection and mutual respect within his family.

c) Maya focuses on practising mindful communication during her interactions with friends and acquaintances throughout the day. During a phone call with a friend, she listens attentively to their updates and experiences, refraining from checking her phone or multitasking. When her friend expresses their worries about an upcoming challenge, Maya responds with empathy and encouragement, offering support and understanding. Throughout their conversation, she embraces moments of silence, allowing herself and her friend to process their thoughts and emotions more intensely. Maya reflects on her experiences with mindful communication and feels grateful for the meaningful connections she cultivated through intentional listening and thoughtful speech.

By actively practising mindful communication, you are not only enhancing the quality of your interactions but also fostering deeper connections with others. This activity serves as a powerful tool to cultivate empathy, understanding, and respect in your relationships. Moreover, it allows you to recognise the transformative power of silence in promoting mutual understanding and connection, inspiring you to continue on this path of self-improvement.

Day 12:

Finding Stillness Within

Activity Summary: Engage in a transformative 15-minute body scan meditation. This practice, when done regularly, can help you release tension, cultivate inner stillness, and promote overall well-being.

Day 12 Activity: Practise a Body Scan Meditation

Instructions:

1. Set aside 15 minutes in a quiet, comfortable space where you won't be disturbed. Find a seated position, ensuring your body is fully supported and relaxed.

2. Close your eyes and bring your awareness to your breath. Take a few deep breaths, inhaling deeply through your nose and exhaling slowly through your mouth, releasing any tension or stress with each exhale.

3. Once you feel centred and grounded, embark on a journey through your body. Starting from your toes, embark on a slow ascent through each part of your body, paying attention to any areas of tension, discomfort, or sensation.

4. As you focus on each body part, consciously relax and release any tension you may be holding. Visualise each muscle and joint becoming soft and supple, melting away stress or tightness.

5. Scan upward through your legs, hips, abdomen, chest, arms, shoulders, neck, and head. Take time with each body part, allowing yourself to relax with each breath.

6. If you encounter any areas of particular tension or discomfort, pause and linger there for a moment. Direct your breath into that area, imagining it expanding and releasing with each inhalation and exhalation.

7. As you complete the body scan, take a few moments to simply rest in stillness and observe any sensations that arise within your body and mind. Reflect on this experience and

allow yourself to fully embrace the peace and tranquillity that comes with being present in the moment.

8. When ready, gently bring your awareness back to your surroundings. Wiggle your fingers and toes, stretch your body if needed, and slowly open your eyes.

9. Take a few more deep breaths, expressing gratitude for this time you've dedicated to nurturing your inner stillness and well-being.

Real-Life Examples

a) Emily sets aside 15 minutes during her lunch break to practise a body scan meditation in her office. She finds a quiet corner, closes her office door, and settles into a comfortable chair. Starting from her toes, she methodically scans through each part of her body, releasing tension and inviting relaxation with each breath. As she reaches her shoulders and neck, where she often holds stress, she takes extra time to breathe deeply and consciously release any tightness. By the end of the meditation, Emily feels a profound sense of calm and rejuvenation, ready to tackle the rest of her day with renewed energy and clarity.

b) David practises a body scan meditation in the evening before bed to unwind and prepare for sleep. He lies down on his yoga mat in his bedroom, dimming the lights and setting a soothing instrumental music track to play softly in the background. Beginning with his toes, he systematically moves through each part of his body, allowing himself to relax and release any tension or worries from the day. By the time he reaches his head, David feels a deep sense of peace and stillness enveloping him, paving the way for a restful night's sleep.

c) Maria incorporates a body scan meditation into her morning routine to start her day on a calm and centred note. After waking up, she sits upright on her meditation cushion in her living room, surrounded by plants and natural light. With her eyes closed, Maria guides her awareness through each part of her body, gently releasing any tightness or discomfort she encounters. As she completes the meditation, Maria feels a profound sense of inner stillness and clarity, setting a positive tone for the day ahead.

By dedicating time to practise a body scan meditation, you are not only cultivating a deeper connection with your body but also releasing tension and stress. This practice can lead you to tap into a profound sense of inner stillness and well-being, a state that can be elusive in the busyness of daily life. Embrace this activity as a powerful tool to nurture yourself and find peace within.

Day 13:

Silence in Movement

Activity Summary: Engage in a physical activity without any background noise. Whether it's yoga, tai chi, or a mindful walk, allow silence to accompany your movement.

Day 13 Activity: Engage in Mindful Physical Activity

Instructions:

1. Choose a physical activity you enjoy, allowing you to move mindfully and intentionally. Examples include yoga, tai chi, qigong, a mindful walk, or any other form of gentle movement that resonates with you.

2. Find a quiet and peaceful environment to engage in your chosen activity without background noise or distractions. This could be indoors or outdoors, depending on your preference and space availability.

3. Begin your practice by taking moments to centre yourself and connect with your breath. Close your eyes and take several deep, conscious breaths, allowing yourself to arrive fully in the present moment.

4. Once you feel grounded and centred, begin your chosen physical activity, focusing on mindfulness and awareness. Pay attention to the sensations in your body as you move, noticing the subtle nuances of each movement and posture.

5. Let go of any distractions or thoughts that arise in your mind, and instead, direct your attention inward to the experience of moving in silence. Allow yourself to fully immerse in the present moment, tuning into the rhythm of your breath and the sensations of your body.

6. If you're practising yoga or tai chi, move through your poses or sequences gracefully and fluently, allowing each movement to flow seamlessly into the next. If you're taking a mindful walk, focus on the sensation of your feet making

contact with the ground, the rhythm of your steps, and the sights and sounds of nature around you.

7. Maintaining a gentle and compassionate attitude toward yourself throughout your practice, honouring your body's limitations and needs. If you encounter any areas of tension or discomfort, breathe into them and allow them to soften and release with each breath.

8. As you near the end of your practice, take a few moments to pause and reflect on how you feel physically and mentally. Notice any shifts or changes in your state of being, and allow yourself to savour the peace and calm from moving in silence.

9. When you're ready, gradually bring your practice to a close, taking a few final breaths to seal the benefits of your mindful movement experience. Express gratitude to yourself for dedicating this time to nurture your body, mind, and spirit.

Real-Life Examples

a) Sarah starts her day with a silent yoga practice in her living room. She rolls out her yoga mat, lights a candle, and says her favourite affirmations to set the mood. As she moves through her sun salutations and standing poses, Sarah focuses on her breath and the sensation of her body moving in space. She feels a deep sense of peace and connection with herself and is grateful for the opportunity to start her day with mindful movement.

b) Mark takes a mindful walk in the park during his lunch break to break up his day and recharge his energy. He leaves his phone behind and tunes into the sights, sounds, and sensations of nature around him. As Mark walks, he focuses on his breath and the feeling of his feet making contact with the earth. He feels more grounded and present with each step, enjoying the simple pleasure of moving in silence.

c) Emma practises tai chi in her backyard as the sun sets, using the quiet evening hours to unwind and relax. She moves through her tai chi form gracefully and precisely, letting go of any stress or tension from the day. With each flowing movement, Emma feels a sense of serenity and tranquillity wash over her, grateful for the healing power of silent movement.

By engaging in mindful physical activity in silence, you can cultivate a deeper connection with your body, quiet your mind, and nourish your spirit. Use this activity as an opportunity to move with intention and presence, savouring the peace and stillness from being fully immersed in the present moment.

Day 14:

Silent Retreat

Activity Summary: Dedicate half a day to a silent retreat. Disconnect from technology and spend time in nature or a quiet indoor space, focusing on inner reflection.

Day 14 Activity: Half-Day of Inner Reflection

Instructions:

1. Choose a suitable location for your silent retreat. This could be a peaceful spot in nature, such as a park, garden, or forest, or a quiet indoor space, like a meditation room, library, or your own home.

2. Begin by disconnecting from all technology and external distractions. Turn off your phone, computer, and any other electronic devices that may disrupt your silence and solitude. Create a sacred space where you can fully immerse yourself in the experience of inner reflection.

3. Set aside at least half a day for your silent retreat. This extended period will allow you to deepen your practice and explore your inner landscape with greater depth and clarity.

4. Find a comfortable seated position on the ground with a cushion or on a chair, and close your eyes. Take several deep breaths to centre yourself and calm your mind, allowing tension or stress to melt away with each exhale.

5. Once you feel grounded and centred, begin your silent retreat by tuning into your inner experience. Notice any thoughts, feelings, or sensations that arise within you, observing them with gentle curiosity and non-judgmental awareness.

6. Allow yourself to fully surrender to the present moment, letting go of any attachments to past or future concerns. Embrace the stillness and silence surrounding you, allowing it to envelop you like a warm blanket of peace and tranquillity.

7. If you're outdoors, connect with the natural world around you. Notice the sights, sounds, and smells of your surroundings, allowing yourself to be fully present and engaged with the beauty of nature.

8. If indoors, create a serene atmosphere by lighting candles, burning incense, or playing soft instrumental music. Surround yourself with objects that inspire a sense of calm and serenity, such as plants, crystals, or meaningful artwork.

Practice deep listening to your inner voice and intuition throughout your silent retreat. Allow yourself to receive any insights, wisdom, or guidance from the depths of your being, trusting in your inner knowing.

As you near the end of your silent retreat, take a few moments to express gratitude for this sacred time of inner reflection and self-discovery. Thank yourself for honouring your need for silence and solitude and for the profound gifts it has bestowed upon you.

Real-Life Examples

a) Daniel spends his silent retreat in a secluded cabin in the mountains, surrounded by towering trees and the soothing sounds of nature. He spends the morning meditating, journaling, and practising yoga, fully immersing himself in the experience of inner reflection. In the afternoon, he takes a quiet walk through the forest, marvelling at the beauty of the natural world and feeling a deep connection with all of life.

b) Maya creates her silent retreat in the comfort of her own home, transforming her living room into a sacred sanctuary for inner reflection. She lights candles, burns sage, and plays soft ambient music to set the mood. Throughout the day, she engages in silent meditation, breathwork, and creative expression, tapping into her intuition and allowing herself to be guided by her inner wisdom and deep subconscious. As the sun sets, Maya feels a profound sense of peace and renewal wash over her, grateful for the opportunity to reconnect with herself in silence.

c) Jamal chooses to spend his silent retreat at a nearby Mosque, seeking the guidance and support of the resident Imam. He participates in silent prayer services, walks the prayer hall in contemplative silence, and reflects quietly in the Mosque courtyard. In the company of like-minded seekers, Jamal feels a deep sense of spiritual communion and community, knowing he is not alone on his journey of inner transformation.

Dedicating half a day to a silent retreat can create a sacred space for inner reflection, self-discovery, and spiritual renewal. Use this time to reconnect with yourself on a deeper level and to cultivate a sense of peace, clarity, and inner harmony.

Day 15:

Silent Journaling

Activity Summary: Spend 30 minutes journaling in complete silence. Write about your thoughts, feelings, and experiences without any distractions.

Day 15 Activity: Reflective Writing in Serenity

Instructions:

1. Find a quiet and comfortable space to focus without interruption. This could be a cosy corner of your home, a tranquil outdoor setting, or any place you feel at ease and free from distractions.

2. Settle into your chosen space and take a few moments to centre yourself. Close your eyes, take a deep breath, and allow your body and mind to relax. Let go of any tension or stress you may be holding onto, and prepare to enter a state of calm and introspection.

3. Open your journal or notebook and begin writing once you feel grounded and centred. Let your thoughts flow freely onto the page without censoring or judging them. Write about whatever comes to mind, whether it's your thoughts, feelings, experiences, or reflections on the day.

4. Embrace the silence as you write, allowing it to deepen your connection with yourself and your innermost thoughts. Pay attention to the rhythm of your breath and the sensations in your body as you put pen to paper. Let the silence envelop you like a comforting blanket, creating a sense of peace and stillness within.

5. As you journal, allow yourself to explore whatever arises with curiosity and compassion. Notice any patterns or themes that emerge in your writing, and use this as an opportunity for self-discovery and insight. Be gentle with yourself as you navigate your inner landscape, and remember that there are no right or wrong answers in this process.

6. If you find your mind wandering or distracted, gently bring your focus back to your writing. Put words on paper as an anchor to keep you grounded in the present moment. Allow the silence to guide you deeper into your thoughts and emotions, revealing hidden truths and insights.

7. If you feel inspired, write for at least 30 minutes or longer. Allow yourself to fully immerse in the experience of silent journaling, letting go of any expectations or pressures to perform. Trust that this entire process is valuable and that you are gaining more profound understanding and clarity with each word you write.

Real-Life Examples

a) Sarah sits beneath a shady tree in her backyard, surrounded by the soothing sounds of nature. With her journal, she begins to write about her recent struggles and challenges, allowing herself to express her thoughts and feelings without inhibition. As she writes, she feels a sense of relief and release, knowing she has a safe space to explore her innermost thoughts in silence.

b) David finds a quiet corner in his favourite coffee shop, away from the hustle and bustle of the city streets. With a steaming cup of coffee beside him, he opens his journal and begins to write about his hopes, dreams, and aspirations for the future. As he delves deeper into his writing, he feels a sense of clarity and purpose emerging from the silence, guiding him towards his goals with renewed determination and focus.

c) Maria retreats to her bedroom after a long day at work, seeking solace in the serenity of her sanctuary. With soft music playing in the background, she opens her journal and begins to write about her gratitude for the blessings in her life. As she writes, she feels a deep sense of peace and contentment wash over her, knowing she can create beauty and meaning through silent journaling.

By spending 30 minutes journaling in complete silence, you can tap into the wisdom of your innermost thoughts and feelings, gaining deeper insight into yourself and your life. Use this time to reflect, process, and express yourself authentically, knowing that silence is critical to unlocking your innermost truths.

Day 16:

Silence in Art

Activity Summary: Visit an art gallery or museum and observe the artwork silently. Allow yourself to be inspired by the beauty and depth of each piece.

Day 16 Activity: Contemplative Observation of Artistic Expressions

Instructions:

1. Choose an art gallery or museum that resonates with you and offers a diverse selection of artwork. Research online or ask for recommendations to find a venue that aligns with your interests and preferences.

2. Plan your visit when the gallery or museum is likely less crowded, allowing you to immerse yourself fully in the experience without distractions. Consider visiting during off-peak hours or weekdays to enjoy a quieter and more contemplative atmosphere.

3. Upon arriving at the art venue, take a few moments to centre yourself and prepare for your silent observation. Find a comfortable spot to sit or stand in front of the artwork without feeling rushed or crowded. Allow yourself to adjust to the surroundings and tune into the energy of the space.

4. Once you feel ready, begin exploring the artwork, moving from one piece to the next at your own pace. Take your time to observe each piece closely, paying attention to the details, colours, textures, and emotions conveyed by the artist.

5. As you engage with each piece, allow yourself to enter a state of silent contemplation, allowing the artwork to speak with you in its language. Notice how it makes you feel, what thoughts and associations arise, and how it resonates with your experiences and perspectives.

6. Resist the urge to analyse or interpret the artwork intellectually; instead, allow yourself to experience it

on a deeper, more intuitive level. Trust your instincts and emotions as you connect with the art, letting go of preconceived notions or expectations.

7. Take breaks as needed to rest and recharge, but spend at least 30 minutes to an hour in silent observation of the artwork. Allow yourself to fully immerse in the experience, surrendering to the beauty and mystery of the artistic expressions before you.

Real-Life Examples

a) Sarah visits a contemporary art gallery in her city, drawn to the abstract paintings' vibrant colours and bold compositions. As she wanders through the gallery, she takes her time to study each artwork up close, appreciating the intricate brushwork and layers of texture. In the gallery's silence, she feels a sense of peace and intrigue, allowing her to connect deeply with the emotions and energy conveyed by the artwork.

b) David explores a classical art museum, captivated by the timeless beauty and elegance of the sculptures and portraits adorning the walls. As he moves from room to room, he loses himself in the silent dialogue between the artist and the viewer, feeling moved by the stories and emotions captured in each masterpiece. In the stillness of the museum, he finds solace and inspiration, renewing his appreciation for the power of art to transcend language and touch the soul.

c) Maria visits a photography exhibition featuring striking images of landscapes, people, and everyday moments captured by talented photographers worldwide. As she gazes at each photograph, she allows herself to be transported to different places and times, feeling deeply connected and empathised with the subjects and scenes depicted. In the silence of the exhibition hall, she experiences a profound sense of unity and interconnectedness, realising the universal language of visual storytelling that binds us all together.

By silently observing artwork in a gallery or museum, you can tap into the beauty, depth, and meaning of artistic expressions, allowing them to inspire and enrich your life journey. Use this opportunity to connect with the emotions, stories, and energy conveyed by the artwork and be transformed by the silent dialogue between the artist and the viewer.

Day 17:

Practising Gratitude in Silence

Activity Summary: Practise silent gratitude meditation for 20 minutes. Reflect on all the things you're grateful for without speaking or writing them down.

Day 17 Activity: Silent Gratitude Meditation

Instructions:

1. Find a quiet and comfortable space to sit up without distractions. Create a serene environment by dimming the lights, lighting a candle, or playing soft instrumental music if desired. Ensure that you won't be interrupted during your meditation session.

2. Get into a relaxed and comfortable position, sitting on a cushion with your legs crossed or sitting on a chair with your arms by your sides. Close your eyes gently and take a few deep breaths to centre yourself and calm your mind.

3. Begin by focusing on your breath, which serves as an anchor to the present moment. Allow each inhale and exhale to flow naturally and rhythmically. Notice the sensation of the breath as it enters and leaves your body, grounding you in the present moment.

4. Once you feel centred and grounded, embark on your personal journey of gratitude. Without speaking or writing anything down, silently reflect on all the things you're grateful for in your life. Start with the simple things, like the air you breathe, the food you eat, and the roof over your head. Then, gradually expand your awareness to include other aspects of your life, such as your relationships, accomplishments, and experiences. This is your unique path of gratitude, and it's a journey only you can take.

5. As you contemplate each aspect of your life with gratitude, allow yourself to fully experience the feelings of appreciation and joy that arise within you. You might also experience other emotions, such as sadness or longing. This

is normal and part of the process. Notice how gratitude fills your heart with warmth and positivity, uplifting your spirit and nourishing your soul.

6. Resist the urge to label or analyse your feelings of gratitude and instead observe them with an open and accepting attitude. Embrace the sensations and emotions that arise during your meditation, allowing them to flow freely without judgement or resistance.

7. Continue to focus on gratitude for the duration of your meditation session, letting your heart expand with love and appreciation for the abundance that surrounds you. If your mind wanders or distractions arise, which is normal, gently bring your focus back to gratitude. You can use your breath as an anchor to keep you grounded in the present moment. Simply observe the distraction, acknowledge it, and then gently guide your attention back to your breath and the feeling of gratitude.

8. When you feel ready, slowly bring your meditation to a close by taking a few deep breaths and gently opening your eyes. Take a moment to express gratitude for the opportunity to practise silent gratitude meditation. As you transition back into your day, carry the positive energy and feelings of gratitude with you. This can be as simple as taking a moment to appreciate the beauty around you or expressing gratitude to someone in your life. By doing so, you extend the benefits of your meditation practice into your daily life.

Real-Life Examples

a) James settles into his meditation space, closing his eyes and taking a few deep breaths to relax his body and mind.

As he begins his silent gratitude meditation, he starts by acknowledging the simple blessings in his life, like the warmth of the sun on his skin and the gentle breeze rustling through the trees outside his window. With each passing moment, he expands his awareness to include his loving family, supportive friends, and fulfilling career. As he basks in the glow of gratitude, James feels a profound sense of contentment and peace wash over him, filling him with renewed energy and optimism. Keep in mind that some days, it might be more challenging to focus on gratitude. That's okay. The practice is about being present and accepting whatever comes up for you.

c) Sarah sits cross-legged on her meditation cushion, closing her eyes and connecting with her breath. As she delves into her silent gratitude meditation, she recalls the challenges she's overcome and the lessons she's learned along the way. With each breath, Sarah fills her heart with gratitude for the strength and resilience that have carried her through difficult times and the growth and transformation that have emerged from adversity. As she continues to reflect on the blessings in her life, Sarah feels a deep sense of gratitude welling up within her, filling her with a profound sense of peace and appreciation for the richness of her experiences.

d) David lies down on his yoga mat, closing his eyes and focusing on his breath as he prepares for his silent gratitude meditation. As he dives into his practice, he brings to mind the countless blessings that fill his life, from the love of his family and friends to the beauty of the natural world surrounding him. With each passing moment, David feels his heart expanding with gratitude, radiating outwards and touching everyone and everything around him. As he basks in the warm glow of appreciation, David feels a sense of interconnectedness and belonging that fills him with profound joy and contentment.

By practising silent gratitude meditation, you can unlock the transformative power of gratitude. This power can cultivate a deeper appreciation for the abundance surrounding you, fostering a greater sense of well-being and fulfilment in your life. Use this opportunity to connect with the blessings in your life without speaking or writing them down, allowing yourself to experience the profound and positive changes that gratitude can bring, all in the silence of your own mind.

Day 18:

Silence and Self-Care

Activity Summary: Indulge in a silent self-care ritual, such as taking a long bath, pampering with skincare, or enjoying a quiet cup of tea.

Day 18 Activity: Nurturing Yourself in Silence: Silent Self-Care Ritual

Instructions:

1. Set aside dedicated time for your silent self-care ritual. Choose a time to immerse yourself in the experience without interruptions or distractions fully.

2. It is crucial to select a self-care activity that deeply connects with you and fosters relaxation and rejuvenation. This could involve immersing yourself in a long bath with calming essential oils, treating your skin with a pampering skincare routine, or enjoying a peaceful cup of herbal tea while engrossed in a book.

3. Create a serene environment for your self-care ritual. Dim the lights, play soft music or nature sounds, and light candles or diffuse calming essential oils to enhance the ambience.

4. Begin your self-care ritual by taking a few deep breaths to centre yourself and calm your mind. Close your eyes and fully relax into the present moment, releasing any tension or stress you may be holding onto.

5. Engage in your chosen self-care activity mindfully and intentionally, focusing on each sensation and experience as it unfolds. Pay attention to the texture of the bathwater or skincare products on your skin, the aroma of the tea as you sip it slowly, or the words on the book's pages as you immerse yourself in the story.

6. Practice silence during your self-care ritual, allowing yourself to fully experience the moment without the need

for external stimulation or distractions. This is a powerful rejuvenation tool, enabling you to fully immerse yourself in the present moment and recharge your mind, body, and soul. Embrace the stillness and tranquillity of the present moment, allowing it to nourish and replenish you.

7. As you engage in your self-care ritual, cultivate deep self-love, compassion, and gratitude for yourself and your body. This is a crucial part of the process, as it helps you to truly honour and appreciate your need for rest, relaxation, and rejuvenation. By treating yourself with kindness and gentleness, you acknowledge your worth and the importance of your well-being.

8. Once you've completed your self-care ritual, take a few moments to reflect on your experience. Notice any shifts or changes in your mood, energy levels, or overall well-being. Express gratitude for the opportunity to nurture yourself in silence and carry the positive energy with you as you continue your day.

Real-Life Examples

a) Emily fills her bathtub with warm water and adds a few drops of lavender essential oil to create a soothing aroma. As she settles into the tub, she closes her eyes and focuses on her breath, allowing herself to release any tension or stress she's been carrying. She takes her time soaking in the warm water, feeling it envelop her body in comfort and relaxation. After her bath, Emily wraps herself in a fluffy towel and spends a few moments in silence, savouring the tranquillity and peace that washes over her.

b) Michael sets up a cosy corner in his living room with a comfortable chair, a soft blanket, and a steaming cup of chamomile tea. He sits and wraps himself in the blanket, sipping his tea slowly and enjoying the soothing warmth that fills him from the inside out. As he savours the quiet moment, Michael reflects on the importance of self-care and taking time to nurture himself in silence. He feels grateful for the opportunity to pause and recharge, knowing that it will help him show up as his best self in all areas of his life.

c) Sarah spreads out her skincare products on her bathroom counter, creating a mini spa experience for herself. She cleanses her face with a gentle cleanser, applies a nourishing face mask, and massages her skin with a luxurious facial oil. As she moves through her skincare routine, Sarah focuses on each step mindfully, appreciating the sensation of her fingers gliding across her skin and the subtle scents of the products. After completing her routine, Sarah takes a moment to gaze in the mirror, noticing the soft glow radiating from her skin and the sense of inner calm that shines in her eyes. She smiles at her reflection, feeling grateful for the opportunity to care for herself in silence and nurture her inner and outer beauty.

Day 19:

Silent Reading

Activity Summary: Engage in the enriching practice of spending 1 hour reading a book in complete silence. This immersive experience enhances your understanding and enjoyment of the book, while also providing a peaceful and rejuvenating escape from daily distractions.

Day 19 Activity: Immerse Yourself in Silent Reading: Silent Reading Session

Instructions:

1. Choose a book you've meant to read or one you've been looking forward to diving into. Select a comfortable and quiet spot to read without interruptions or distractions.

2. Set aside one hour for your silent reading session. Turn off electronic devices, silence notifications, and create a peaceful environment conducive to deep concentration and immersion in the book.

3. Begin your silent reading session by taking deep breaths to centre yourself and clear your mind. Then, open the book and allow yourself to become fully absorbed in the story, characters, and imagery.

4. Read at your own pace, savouring each word and sentence as you progress through the pages. Pay attention to the author's writing style, descriptive language, and narrative flow. Do your best to relate to the world of the book.

5. Engage with the text mindfully, visualising scenes in your mind's eye, empathising with the character's emotions, and reflecting on the themes and messages conveyed by the story.

6. Embrace moments of silence between paragraphs or chapters, allowing yourself to pause and absorb the content before continuing. Use these pauses to reflect on your reading experience and connect with the deeper meanings and insights within the book.

7. As you read, notice any thoughts or distractions that arise and gently bring your focus back to the present moment and the book before you. Practise staying fully present and engaged with the text, letting go of any worries or concerns outside the reading experience.

8. After one hour has passed, take a moment to reflect on your silent reading session. This reflection will help you to internalise the content and make the reading experience more meaningful. Notice how you feel mentally, emotionally, and physically after immersing yourself in the book. Express gratitude for the opportunity to escape into the world of literature and nourish your mind with the power of storytelling. Feel a sense of accomplishment and fulfilment from dedicating this time to your personal enrichment and relaxation.

Real-Life Examples

a) Julia curls up on her favourite armchair with a cup of tea and a captivating novel she's been eager to read. As she opens the book and begins to read, she feels drawn into the story, losing track of time as she becomes engrossed in the characters' lives and adventures. With each page turn, Julia feels a sense of excitement and anticipation, eager to uncover what happens next in the plot. As the hour ends, she closes the book with a satisfied sigh, feeling grateful for the opportunity to escape into the world of literature and recharge her mind.

b) David seizes his lunch break to enjoy some quiet time reading in the park. He finds a tranquil spot under a tree, spreads a blanket, and opens his book to the first page. As he reads, he feels the stress and busyness of the day dissolve, replaced by a profound sense of calm and relaxation. The sounds of nature provide a soothing backdrop to his reading experience, deepening his connection to the story and characters. When the hour is up, David closes the book reluctantly, feeling refreshed and rejuvenated from his time immersed in silent reading. He steps back into his day with a renewed sense of energy and focus.

c) During his silent reading session, Alex opts for a thought-provoking non-fiction book. As he delves into the pages, he is captivated by the author's insights and perspectives. He takes notes in the margins, underlining key passages and jotting down his thoughts and reflections as he reads. The hour seems to fly by as Alex engages deeply with the material, gaining new insights and expanding his understanding of the subject matter. As he closes the book, he feels inspired and intellectually stimulated, grateful for the opportunity to engage in silent reading and enrich his mind with new knowledge. He carries this inspiration and new knowledge with him, ready to apply it in his daily life.

Day 20:

Silent Mindfulness

Activity Summary: Practise silent mindfulness throughout the day. Pay attention to each moment as it unfolds without judgement or commentary.

Day 20 Activity: Cultivating Silent Mindfulness: Silent Mindfulness Practice

Instructions:

1. Begin your day with the intention of practising silent mindfulness, a state of heightened awareness and presence in each moment. Set the intention to observe your thoughts, emotions, and sensations without judgement or commentary.

2. Engage in your daily activities with mindfulness and attention to the present moment. Whether eating breakfast, commuting to work, or completing tasks, strive to be fully present and aware of each action you perform.

3. As you go about your day, pay close attention to your breath as an anchor for mindfulness. Take deep, intentional breaths to ground yourself in the present moment whenever you feel distracted or overwhelmed.

4. Notice the sensations in your body as you move, sit, or stand. Tune into the feeling of your feet touching the ground, the rhythm of your breath, and the sensations of movement as you go about your daily activities.

5. Practise silent observation of your surroundings, noticing the sights, sounds, and smells around you without getting caught up in thoughts or judgments. Allow yourself to be fully immersed in the present moment and appreciate the richness of your sensory experience.

6. Throughout the day, check in with yourself regularly to assess your level of mindfulness. Notice moments when your mind wanders or becomes caught up in thoughts, and gently guide your attention back to the present moment.

7. Embrace moments of silence and stillness throughout the day, allowing yourself to be without the need for constant stimulation or distraction. Use these moments to reconnect with yourself and cultivate inner peace and calm.

8. At the end of the day, reflect on your experience with silent mindfulness. Notice any shifts in your awareness, mood, or overall well-being from practising mindfulness throughout the day.

Real-Life Examples

a) Sarah starts her day with a silent mindfulness practice as she sips her morning coffee. Instead of rushing through her breakfast, she takes the time to savour each sip, noticing the warmth of the mug in her hands and the rich aroma of the coffee. As she commutes to work, she observes her surroundings silently, noticing the colours of the sky, the sounds of traffic, and the feel of the breeze on her skin. Throughout the day, Sarah takes regular breaks to check in with her breath and bring her attention back to the present moment. By the end of the day, she feels more grounded, centred, and at peace.

b) John incorporates silent mindfulness into his daily routine by practising mindful walking during his lunch break. As he strolls through the park near his office, he focuses on each step, feeling the earth beneath his feet and the rhythm of his breath. He takes in the sights and sounds of nature around him, noticing the rustle of leaves in the wind and birds chirping overhead. With each mindful step, John feels more connected to himself and the world around him, experiencing a sense of calm and clarity.

c) Maria practises silent mindfulness while completing household chores in the evening. Instead of rushing through her tasks, she approaches each one with mindfulness and attention to detail. As Maria washes dishes, she focuses on the sensation of water on her hands and soap bubbles popping. When folding laundry, she takes the time to appreciate the texture and smell of freshly washed clothes. By the end of the evening, Maria feels more present, relaxed, and content with the simple moments of her day.

Day 21:

Reflecting on Progress

Activity Summary: Reflect on your journey with silence so far. Notice any changes in your mood, energy levels, or overall well-being.

Day 21 Activity: Reflecting on Your Silence Journey Progress

Instructions:

1. Set aside dedicated time for reflection on your journey with silence. Find a quiet and comfortable space to be alone with your thoughts.

2. It's essential to review your experiences with silence since you started this journey. Consider the activities you've practised, the insights you've gained, and any challenges you've encountered. This reflection will provide valuable insights into your personal growth and areas where you can improve.

3. It's important to take note of any changes you've noticed in your mood, energy levels, or overall well-being since incorporating silence into your daily life. Pay attention to subtle shifts and significant transformations. This will help you understand the impact of silence on your mental and emotional health.

4. Reflect on how your relationship with silence has evolved over the past few weeks. Have you developed a deeper appreciation for moments of stillness? Are you more aware of the impact of noise and distraction on your mental and emotional state?

5. Consider the lessons you've learned from your experiences with silence. Have you discovered new ways to cultivate inner peace and calm? Are you better equipped to manage stress and navigate challenges in your daily life?

6. Take stock of any insights or realisations that have emerged from your practice of silence. Have you gained clarity on certain aspects of your life or a deeper understanding of yourself and your values?

7. Acknowledge and celebrate your progress on this journey. Recognise the courage and commitment you've shown to embrace silence in a world of noise and distraction. Take pride in prioritising your well-being and nurturing your inner peace. You've come a long way, and your dedication to this practice is something to be truly proud of.

8. Consider setting intentions or goals for the next phase of your silence journey. Are there areas where you'd like to deepen your practice or explore new aspects of silence? Take this opportunity to chart your course for continued growth and discovery.

Real-Life Examples

a) Emily sits down with her journal to reflect on her journey with silence over the past three weeks. As she flips through the pages, she notices how her entries have evolved from simple observations to more profound reflections on the meaning of silence in her life. She recalls the challenges she faced initially, such as quieting her racing thoughts during meditation and the sense of accomplishment she experienced as she gradually learned to embrace moments of stillness. Emily is amazed by the positive changes in her mood and energy levels since incorporating silence into her daily routine. She feels more centred, grounded, and resilient during stressful situations. Moving forward, Emily intends to deepen her silent meditation practice and explore new ways to integrate silence into her work and relationships.

b) David takes a quiet walk in nature, reflecting on his journey with silence. As he wanders through the forest, he recalls the moments of clarity and insight he's experienced while practising silent contemplation. He marvels at how much he's learned about himself and the world through his encounters with silence. David acknowledges his challenges, such as resisting the urge to fill every moment with noise or distraction. Still, he's grateful for the growth and transformation from embracing moments of stillness. Looking ahead, David resolves to continue nurturing his connection with silence and exploring its profound gifts.

c) Sarah sits by the window with a cup of tea, gazing out at the quiet street below as she reflects on her silent journey. She recalls the scepticism she felt initially, wondering how silence could make a difference in her busy life. But as she immersed herself in practice, Sarah discovered a profound sense of inner peace and tranquillity she hadn't known before. She marvels at the subtle shifts in her perspective and the newfound clarity that has emerged from moments of silence. Sarah feels a deep gratitude for the opportunity to explore the transformative power of silence, and she looks forward to continuing her journey with an open heart and mind, knowing that it will always bring her back to this serene state.

Day 22:

Sharing Silence

Activity Summary: Practise silent communication with a loved one or friend. Spend time together without speaking, focusing on non-verbal cues and connection.

Day 22 Activity: Practice Silent Communication with a Loved One

Instructions:

1. Choose a loved one or friend whom you feel comfortable sharing silence with. This could be a family member or a close friend.

2. Set aside dedicated time to spend together in silence. Find a quiet and comfortable space where you won't be disturbed.

3. Begin by sitting or standing near each other. Make eye contact and take a few deep breaths to centre yourselves in the present moment.

4. Let go of any expectations or assumptions about what silent communication should look like. Instead, focus on being fully present with each other and open to whatever arises.

5. Allow yourselves to communicate non-verbally through gestures, facial expressions, and body language. Pay attention to the subtle cues and signals that convey meaning without words.

6. Engage in activities encouraging shared silence, such as taking a leisurely walk together, enjoying a meal in silence, or simply sitting together and observing the world around you.

7. Notice how it feels to communicate without words. Pay attention to the depth of connection that can be cultivated through shared silence and any challenges or discomfort that may arise.

8. After the designated period of silent communication, take a moment to reflect on your experience together. Share your thoughts, feelings, and observations, acknowledging the unique bond that silence can foster.

Real-Life Examples

a) Sarah and her husband, Alex, decided to practise silent communication during their evening walk in the park. As they stroll hand in hand along the winding paths, they relish the opportunity to connect without words. Sarah notices Alex squeezing her hand gently when he sees a stunning flower, and she returns the gesture with a smile. They pause by a tranquil pond to watch the ducks gliding across the water, sharing a moment of quiet awe at the beauty of nature. After their walk, they sit on a bench together, gazing up at the stars overhead and feeling a profound connection that transcends language.

b) David and his teenage daughter, Maya, practise silent communication at home for an afternoon. They turn off their phones and other electronic devices, creating a peaceful sanctuary free from distractions. They sit together in the living room, each engrossed in their silent activities—David reading a book and Maya sketching in her notebook. Despite the absence of words, they feel a deep sense of closeness and understanding between them. As the afternoon unfolds, they exchange occasional smiles and nods, silently affirming their bond as father and daughter.

c) Emily and her best friend, Sarah, embark on a silent mountain hike. They leave their phones behind and immerse themselves in the natural beauty surrounding them. As they trek along the rugged trails, they marvel at the majestic peaks and lush forests, communicating their awe through shared glances and gestures. They sit together silently at a scenic overlook, savouring the panoramic views. As they make their way back down the mountain, they feel a sense of renewal and rejuvenation that can only be found in the embrace of shared silence.

Day 23:

Silent Gratitude Walk

Activity Summary: Take a silent walk outdoors and express gratitude for the beauty of nature. Notice the sights, sounds, and sensations around you without speaking.

Day 23 Activity: Expressing Gratitude in Silence Amidst Nature

Instructions:

1. Choose a time and location for your silent gratitude walk. Opt for a natural setting such as a park, forest trail, beach, or botanical garden where you can immerse yourself in the beauty of nature.

2. Begin your walk by taking a few deep breaths to centre yourself in the present moment. Allow yourself to let go of any distractions or concerns and focus solely on the experience of gratitude and connection with nature.

3. Pay close attention to your surroundings using all your senses as you walk. Notice the vibrant colours of the flowers, the gentle rustle of leaves in the breeze, the warmth of the sunlight on your skin, and the melodic chirping of birds.

4. With each step, express silent gratitude for the abundance and beauty of the natural world. Feel a sense of appreciation for the intricate ecosystem that sustains life and provides endless wonders to behold.

5. Engage in mindful observation, taking time to appreciate the small details and moments of beauty that often go unnoticed in the hustle and bustle of daily life. Notice the delicate patterns in a butterfly's wings, the rhythmic dance of tree branches swaying in the wind, and the soothing rhythm of waves lapping against the shore.

6. Allow yourself to be fully present in the moment, letting go of worries about the past or future. Focus on the simple joy of being alive and surrounded by the majesty of nature.

7. As you continue your walk, cultivate a sense of interconnectedness with the natural world. Recognise that you are part of a vast and intricate web of life, and feel gratitude for the privilege of sharing this planet with countless other beings.

8. After your walk, take a moment to reflect on your experience. Notice any shifts in your mood or mindset, as well as any feelings of peace, contentment, or awe that may have arisen during your time in nature.

Real-Life Examples

a) Sarah embarks on a silent gratitude walk through her local botanical garden. As she meanders along the winding paths, she takes in the breathtaking flowers, trees, and shrubs surrounding her. With each step, Sarah silently expresses gratitude for the vibrant colours, intricate patterns, and delicate fragrances that fill the air. As she pauses by a tranquil pond, she feels a deep connection with the natural world and a profound appreciation for the beauty surrounding her.

b) David takes a silent gratitude walk along the beach near his home. As he walks barefoot in the sand, he feels the warmth of the sun on his skin and the gentle caress of the ocean breeze. With each stride, David silently thanks for the vast expanse of sky above him, the rhythmic ebb and flow of the tide, and the soothing sound of waves crashing against the shore. As he watches the sunset, painting the sky with hues of pink and orange, he feels a sense of peace and surprise, grateful for the beauty of nature's ever-changing canvas.

c) Emily takes silent gratitude and walks through the forest trails near her neighbourhood. As she walks amidst towering trees and dappled sunlight, she feels a sense of awe and reverence for the ancient wisdom and majesty of the forest. With each step, Emily silently expresses gratitude for the abundant life teeming around her – from the chirping of birds overhead to the rustling of small animals in the underbrush. As she reaches a clearing with a panoramic view of the valley below, she feels her heart swell with gratitude for the natural wonders that surround her, grateful for the opportunity to witness such breathtaking beauty.

Day 24:

Silent Listening

Activity Summary: Practise silent listening to a soundscape for 30 minutes. Pay attention to the nuances and textures of the sound without any distractions.

Day 24 Activity: Engaging in Deep Listening Without Distractions

Instructions:

1. Find a quiet and comfortable space to sit without interruptions. Choose a location to immerse yourself in the experience without external distractions.

2. Take a few deep breaths to centre yourself and calm your mind. Allow yourself to let go of any thoughts or worries and prepare to enter a state of deep listening. Remember, it's your journey, so choose a soundscape that truly resonates with you. It could be ambient sounds, nature recordings, animal sounds or any other audio that captures your interest and curiosity.

3. Before you start, take a few deep breaths to centre yourself and calm your mind. This simple act of breathing deeply helps you let go of any thoughts or worries and prepares you to enter a state of deep listening.

4. Start playing the soundscape at a comfortable volume. Close your eyes and focus entirely on the sound, allowing it to wash over you and envelop your senses.

5. As you listen, pay close attention to the nuances and textures of the sound. Notice the interplay of different elements, the variations in tone and pitch, and the subtle shifts in volume and intensity.

6. Engage with the soundscape on a deep level, allowing yourself to become fully absorbed in the auditory experience. It's important to let go of any judgements or expectations,

as this enables the sound to unfold naturally and enhances your listening experience.

7. Notice how your body and mind respond to the soundscape. Listen to any physical sensations, emotions, or thoughts during the listening experience.

8. If your mind begins to wander or you find yourself distracted, remember, it's a normal part of the practice. Gently bring your focus back to the sound and continue listening with intention and curiosity. Each time you do this, you're strengthening your ability to focus and be present.

9. Continue listening for at least 30 minutes, allowing yourself to explore the soundscape's depths fully. Remember, the more you engage in deep listening, the more you nourish your mind, body, and soul. Trust in silence and deep listening to bring you peace and relaxation.

Real-Life Examples

a) James sets aside 30 minutes to listen silently to the sound of ocean waves. As the sound begins to play, he closes his eyes and focuses entirely on the sound. He notices the intricate sounds weaving together, creating a rich tapestry of sound that resonates deeply with him. As the sounds progress, James becomes increasingly immersed in the experience, losing track of time as he allows himself to be carried away by the beauty and complexity of the ocean's sound.

b) Sophia decides to explore silent listening by immersing herself in the sounds of nature. She finds a recording of a forest soundscape and begins to listen intently, closing her eyes to shut out any visual distractions. As birdsong, rustling leaves, and trickling water fill the room, Sophia feels a sense of peace and tranquillity encapsulate her. She imagines herself walking through a lush forest, surrounded by the sights and sounds of the natural world. With each passing minute, Sophia becomes more attuned to the rhythms of nature, feeling a deep connection to the earth and all its wonders.

c) Alex opts for a more experimental approach to silent listening by choosing the minimalist sound of a drum. As the sparse, ethereal sounds fill the room, he allows himself to sink into deep relaxation and receptivity. Without the distractions of lyrics or complex melodies, Alex focuses on the subtle nuances of the drum sound – the gentle thud, the faint echoes of distant percussion, and the soft swells and fades of sound. Alex discovers a profound sense of stillness and clarity in the silence between notes, feeling like he's tapping into something greater than himself.

Day 25:

Silence in Movement

Activity Summary: Engage in a silent physical activity, such as dancing or stretching. Allow your body to move freely without any external noise.

Day 25 Activity: Embracing Stillness in Motion

Instructions:

1. Choose a silent physical activity that resonates with you. It could be dancing, yoga, stretching, or any other form of movement that allows you to connect with your body and breathing.
2. Find a quiet and spacious area where you can move freely without distractions. Turn off any electronic devices and minimise external noise to create a peaceful environment.
3. Take a few deep breaths to centre yourself and prepare for the silent movement practice. Close your eyes if it helps you to focus inward and block out external stimuli.
4. Start moving your body gently and fluidly, allowing each movement to arise naturally from within. Let go of any expectations or judgments and allow yourself to be present in the moment.
5. Tune into your body's sensations as you move, paying attention to the subtle shifts in energy, tension, and relaxation. Notice how your breath synchronises with your movements, guiding you into deep presence and awareness.
6. Allow your movements to flow freely and spontaneously without any predetermined choreography or structure. Trust your body's innate wisdom to guide you as you explore different shapes, gestures, and expressions.
7. Engage your senses in the experience, fully immersing yourself in the present moment. Notice the sensation of your feet touching the ground, the rhythm of your breath,

and the subtle sounds of your body moving through space.
8. Embrace the silence within and around you as you continue to move, allowing it to deepen your connection to yourself and the world around you. Let go of any need for external validation or approval and be with yourself in this sacred moment of movement and stillness.

Real-Life Examples

a) Sarah begins her silent movement practice by rolling out her yoga mat in a sunlit corner of her living room. As she closes her eyes and takes a few deep breaths, she feels a sense of calm wash over her. She starts with gentle stretching, allowing her body to unwind and release any tension from the day. As she transitions into a series of yoga poses, Sarah focuses on the sensation of her breath and the subtle movements of her body. With each pose, she feels more grounded and centred, connecting deeply with her inner self.

b) David decides to explore silent movement through dance, putting on his favourite acapella (music-free) song and letting his body move to the rhythm. As he sways and twirls around the room, he feels a sense of freedom and liberation. Without external distractions, David loses himself in the sounds, allowing them to guide his movements and express his emotions. With each step, he feels alive and connected to the present moment, embracing the joy of silent movement as a form of self-expression and self-discovery.

c) Maria opts for a silent stretching session in her backyard, surrounded by the sounds of nature and the gentle breeze. As she flows through a series of stretching exercises, she feels a deep sense of relaxation and openness in her body. She feels tension melting with each stretch and a sense of spaciousness expanding. As she gazes at the sky, Maria feels a profound sense of connection to the universe, recognizing the beauty and wonder of silent movement as a gateway to inner peace and harmony.

Day 26:

Silent Cooking

Activity Summary: Prepare a meal in complete silence. Focus on the sensations of cooking and the aromas of the food without any background noise.

Day 26 Activity: Nourishing Body and Mind in Silence

Instructions:

1. Choose a recipe you enjoy and gather all the ingredients and kitchen tools. Decide on a meal you can prepare without requiring too much mental effort, allowing you to focus on the experience of cooking in silence.
2. Find a calm and peaceful kitchen area where you can work undisturbed. Turn off electronic devices like TVs or radios to create a silent atmosphere conducive to mindfulness and concentration.
3. Before you begin cooking, take a few moments to centre yourself. Close your eyes and take several deep breaths, allowing yourself to let go of any distractions or worries from the outside world. Set an intention to engage fully in the cooking process and savour each moment of silence.
4. Begin by carefully washing and preparing the ingredients, paying attention to each item's textures, colours, and smells. Allow yourself to fully immerse in the sensory experience of cooking, using all your senses to connect with the food and the present moment.
5. As you chop, slice, and dice the ingredients, focus on the rhythmic movements of your hands and the sound of the knife against the cutting board. Notice the vibrant colours and fragrant aromas that emerge as you prepare the meal, allowing yourself to appreciate the beauty and abundance of nature's bounty.
6. Engage in each step of the cooking process with intention and mindfulness, from sautéing vegetables to simmering

sauces to baking bread. Allow yourself to be fully present in the moment, embracing the simplicity and joy of creating nourishing food with your own hands.

7. Notice how your body and mind feel in the kitchen's silence as the meal takes shape. Pay attention to any sensations of calmness, contentment, or gratitude that arise within you as you cook, savouring the experience of being fully present.

8. Once the meal is ready, take a moment to appreciate your creation before serving it to yourself or others. Notice the finished dish's colours, textures, and aromas, allowing yourself to savour the fruits of your labour in silence fully.

Real-Life Examples

a) Emma decides to prepare a simple pasta dish for her silent cooking activity. As she boils the pasta and chops the vegetables, she focuses on the soothing sounds of bubbling water and the satisfying crunch of fresh produce. She takes her time stirring the sauce and seasoning it with herbs, allowing the flavours to harmonise harmoniously. With each step, Emma feels a sense of peace and fulfilment, grateful for the opportunity to nourish herself and her loved ones with a homemade meal made in silence.

b) Michael chooses to bake cookies for his silent cooking experience. As he mixes the ingredients and shapes the dough into perfect rounds, he savours the comforting aroma of vanilla and chocolate filling the kitchen. He listens to the mixer whirring and the oven door closing, feeling satisfied as he watches the cookies bake to golden perfection. With each cookie that emerges from the oven, Michael feels a profound sense of joy and accomplishment, grateful for the simple pleasure of baking in silence.

c) Sarah opts for a salad for her silent cooking activity, focusing on the ingredients' freshness and vibrancy. As she washes and chops the lettuce, tomatoes, and cucumbers, she revels in each vegetable's crispness and the greens' earthy aroma. She carefully drizzles olive oil and vinegar over the salad, tossing it gently to coat each leaf with dressing. With each bite of the finished salad, Sarah feels a sense of vitality and nourishment, grateful for the opportunity to connect with nature's bounty in silence.

Day 27:

Silent Reflection

Activity Summary: Spend time in silent reflection, contemplating your values, goals, and aspirations. Allow yourself to connect deeply with your innermost desires.

Day 27 Activity: Delving into the Depths of Self-Discovery

Instructions:

1. Find a comfortable and quiet space to engage in silent reflection without distractions. This could be a cosy corner of your home, a peaceful spot in nature, or any other environment where you feel at ease and undisturbed.
2. Sit or lie down in a relaxed position, allowing yourself to settle into a state of calmness and stillness. Close your eyes if it helps you to focus inward, but keep your mind alert and receptive to the process of reflection.
3. Take a few deep breaths to centre yourself and clear your mind of any external thoughts or distractions. Let go of any tension or stress you may be holding onto, allowing yourself to fully relax in the present moment.
4. Begin your silent reflection by contemplating your values, beliefs, and principles. Consider what matters most to you and how these values shape your thoughts, actions, and decisions. Allow yourself to explore the core principles that guide you on your journey of self-discovery.
5. Next, turn your attention to your goals and aspirations, both short-term and long-term. Reflect on what you hope to achieve in various areas of your life, such as career, relationships, health, and personal development. Consider how these goals align with your values and contribute to your fulfilment and purpose.
6. As you delve deeper into your silent reflection, allow yourself to connect with your innermost desires and aspirations. Listen to the whispers of your heart and intuition,

paying attention to any insights or inspirations from within. Trust in your inner wisdom and allow it to guide you on your path of self-discovery.

7. Take your time with this silent reflection, allowing yourself to explore and uncover the depths of your inner being fully. There is no rush or pressure to reach specific conclusions or answers – allow yourself to be present with whatever arises during this process.

8. Once you feel complete with your silent reflection, take a few moments to express gratitude for the insights and revelations you've gained. Acknowledge the power of silence in helping you connect with your inner self and deepen your understanding of who you are and what you truly desire.

Real-Life Examples

a) Rachel sets aside time for silent reflection in the early morning hours before the hustle and bustle of the day begins. Sitting quietly in her favourite armchair, she reflects on her core values of integrity, compassion, and personal growth. She considers how these values influence her decisions and interactions with others and how she can further embody them daily. Rachel also reflects on her long-term goal of starting her nonprofit organisation, envisioning the positive impact she hopes to make in the world through her work.

b) David takes a silent hike in the nearby mountains as part of his reflection practice. As he walks along the winding trails, surrounded by towering trees and sweeping vistas, he contemplates his aspirations for the future. He reflects on his passion for environmental conservation and desire to protect and preserve the natural world for future generations. David also reflects on his personal goals of living a more balanced and purposeful life, finding ways to prioritise his health, relationships, and personal growth amidst the demands of his busy career.

c) Sofia spends silent reflection time journaling in her favourite cosy cafe. As she sips her latte and puts pen to paper, she explores her deepest desires and dreams for the future. She reflects on her values of creativity, authenticity, and connection and how she can infuse these values into her creative endeavours and relationships. Sofia also reflects on her career goals of becoming a successful writer and artist, envisioning the impact she hopes to make through her work and the legacy she hopes to leave behind.

Day 28:

Silent Gratitude Practice

Activity Summary: Engage in the transformative power of silent gratitude throughout the day, silently expressing appreciation for the people, experiences, and blessings in your life. This practice has the potential to shift your perspective and bring about profound changes in your daily life.

Day 28 Activity: Cultivating Appreciation in Silence

Instructions:

1. Begin your day with a moment of silent gratitude as soon as you wake up. Before getting out of bed, take a few deep breaths and silently express appreciation for the gift of a new day, the comfort of your bed, and the opportunity to experience life again.
2. Throughout the day, practise silent gratitude during moments of transition or pause. Whether waiting in line, commuting to work, or taking a short break, take a moment to silently acknowledge and appreciate the people, experiences, and blessings in your life.
3. As you go about your daily activities, cultivate awareness of the little things that bring you joy and comfort. Whether it's the sun's gentle warmth on your face, the comforting aroma of your favourite coffee, or the infectious laughter of loved ones, silently express gratitude for these simple pleasures that enrich your life and bring a smile to your face.
4. During meals, take a moment of silent gratitude before eating to express appreciation for the nourishment and sustenance provided by the food. Reflect on the journey of the food from seed to plate, acknowledging the efforts of farmers, growers, and cooks who have contributed to your meal.
5. Before bedtime, conclude your day with a silent gratitude practice. Reflect on the events, interactions, and experiences of the day, and silently express gratitude for the lessons learned, the connections made, and the shared moments of

joy and laughter.

6. A key aspect of this practice is to maintain an attitude of openness and receptivity to the abundance of blessings surrounding you. This mindset allows you to be present with gratitude, even in challenging moments, knowing that every experience offers growth and learning opportunities.

Real-Life Examples

a) Sarah practises silent gratitude during her morning commute to work. Sitting quietly on the train, she takes a moment to reflect on the people and experiences for which she's grateful. She silently expresses appreciation for her supportive family, her caring friends, and the opportunities she's been given to pursue her passions and interests. Sarah also expresses gratitude for life's simple pleasures, such as the beauty of nature, the kindness of strangers, and the warmth of a smile.

b) James has found that incorporating silent gratitude into his daily mindfulness practice has been transformative. Throughout the day, he takes moments of pause to silently acknowledge and appreciate the abundance of blessings in his life. Whether walking in nature, working at his desk, or spending time with loved ones, James cultivates awareness of the present moment and expresses gratitude for the richness of his experiences. This practice helps him to stay grounded, centred, and connected to the beauty and wonder of life.

c) Maria practises silent gratitude during her evening routine before bed. As she prepares for sleep, she takes a few moments to reflect on the day's events and silently express appreciation for the blessings she's received. She thanks for her family's love and support, the kindness of her co-workers, and the opportunities to learn and grow. Maria also expresses gratitude for the gift of another day lived fully and the promise of new adventures.

Day 29:

Silent Sleep

Activity Summary: Practise silent relaxation techniques before bedtime to promote restful sleep. Avoid screens and distractions, focusing on quieting the mind and body.

Day 29 Activity: Cultivating Peaceful Rest through Silent Relaxation

Instructions:

1. Begin your silent sleep routine by setting aside time before bedtime to unwind and relax. Aim for at least 30 minutes to an hour of quiet time to prepare your mind and body for sleep.
2. Create a calming environment in your bedroom by dimming the lights, minimising noise, and removing distractions such as electronic devices or bright screens. Consider using soft lighting or candles to create a soothing ambience.
3. Practise deep breathing exercises to calm the mind and promote relaxation. Sit or lie down comfortably, close your eyes, and take slow, deep breaths through your nose and out through your mouth. Focus on the sensation of your breath as it enters and leaves your body, allowing yourself to let go of any tension or stress with each exhale.
4. Engage in gentle stretching or progressive muscle relaxation to release physical tension and prepare your body for sleep. Move through stretches or tense-and-release exercises, focusing on different muscle groups from head to toe. Pay attention to any areas of tightness or discomfort, and allow yourself to release tension with each stretch or contraction.
5. Practice mindfulness meditation to quiet the mind and cultivate inner peace. Sit comfortably, close your eyes, and bring your attention to the present moment. Notice any thoughts, feelings, or sensations that arise without

judgement, and gently redirect your focus to your breath whenever your mind wanders.

6. Engage in a relaxing bedtime ritual to signal to your body that it's time to wind down and prepare for sleep. This could include reading a book, taking a warm bath, or listening to calming music. Choose activities that help you feel relaxed and at ease, and avoid stimulating or mentally engaging activities that may interfere with your ability to fall asleep.

7. Practice gratitude and positive affirmations before bed to promote feelings of contentment and relaxation. Take a few moments to reflect on the things you're grateful for and silently express appreciation for the blessings in your life. Repeat affirmations or positive statements to yourself, such as "I am calm, peaceful, and ready for sleep," to reinforce a sense of relaxation and well-being.

Real-Life Examples

a) Emily begins her silent sleep routine by turning off all screens and electronic devices an hour before bedtime. She creates a cosy atmosphere in her bedroom with soft lighting and a calming essential oil diffuser. Emily practises deep breathing exercises and progressive muscle relaxation to release tension from her body and quiet her mind. She then reads a few pages of a book or listens to gentle music to help her relax before drifting off to sleep.

b) Alex incorporates mindfulness meditation into his bedtime routine to promote restful sleep. He spends 15-20 minutes practising mindfulness meditation, focusing on his breath and allowing his thoughts to come and go without attachment. Alex finds that this practice helps to quiet his mind and ease any anxiety or stress he may be feeling. After meditation, he takes a warm shower and practises gratitude by silently expressing appreciation for the day's blessings before turning in for the night.

c) Before bed, Sarah engages in a gentle yoga practice to relax her body and prepare for sleep. She moves through various gentle stretches and restorative poses, focusing on deep breathing and mindful movement. Sarah then practises positive affirmations and gratitude as she settles into bed, silently repeating phrases such as "I am grateful for the peace and tranquillity of this moment" and "I am ready to embrace restful sleep." She drifts to sleep, feeling calm, centred, and ready to recharge for the day ahead.

Day 30:

Celebrating Silence

Activity Summary: Today, we celebrate a significant milestone-the completion of your 30-day journey with silence. This journey has been transformative, providing you with valuable gifts and profound insights. Now, it's time to engage in a period of quiet celebration, reflecting on the journey and its impact on your life.

Day 30 Activity: Embracing Gratitude and Reflection in Quiet Celebration

Instructions:

1. Begin your final day of the 30-day journey by setting aside dedicated time for quiet reflection and celebration. Choose a peaceful and comfortable space to immerse yourself in the moment without distractions fully.
2. Take a few moments to close your eyes, centre yourself, and connect with your breath. Allow yourself to let go of any lingering tension or stress, and embrace a sense of gratitude for the journey you've undertaken over the past month.
3. Reflect on the experiences, insights, and growth you've encountered throughout your 30 days of exploring silence. Consider the physical, emotional, and spiritual benefits you've experienced and any challenges you've overcome.
4. As you reflect, express deep gratitude for the gift of silence and the opportunities it has provided for self-discovery, introspection, and inner peace. Take a moment to acknowledge the stillness and tranquillity that have brought you clarity, inspiration, and a deeper connection to yourself and the world around you.
5. Now, let's celebrate your personal growth and milestones, no matter how small or insignificant they may seem. Reflect on the courage, commitment, and dedication you've demonstrated in embracing silence as a personal growth and transformation tool. Take pride in the changes you've made and the person you've become.
6. Ponder how you can continue to integrate the invaluable

lessons and practices of silence into your daily life as you move forward. Contemplate the habits, routines, and rituals you've nurtured during your 30-day journey, and identify strategies to sustain and expand upon them in the days, weeks, and months to come. Feel hopeful and committed to maintaining the peace and clarity that silence brings.

7. Express gratitude for the opportunity to embark on this journey of self-discovery and renewal and celebrate its profound impact on your life and well-being. Allow yourself to bask in the joy, peace, and fulfilment that come from embracing silence and honouring your sacred space. Feel the serenity and contentment that silence brings.

Real-Life Examples:

a) James begins his final day of the 30-day journey by lighting a candle and sitting in quiet reflection in his favourite corner of his home. He takes a few deep breaths, fully embracing the present moment and letting go of any lingering worries or distractions. James reflects on the lessons he's learned and the growth he's experienced throughout the past month, feeling grateful for the opportunity to explore silence and its transformative power. He takes time to celebrate his achievements and accomplishments, acknowledging the positive changes in his life and the profound impact silence has had on his well-being.

b) Maya spends her final day of the 30-day journey by taking a nature walk in her favourite park. She finds a quiet spot by a tranquil pond, surrounded by the beauty of nature, and takes a moment to connect with her breath and centre herself. Maya reflects on the profound insights and revelations she's gained while exploring silence, feeling inspired and motivated by the clarity, peace, and inspiration it has brought into her life. She celebrates her journey by journaling about her experiences and expressing deep gratitude for the gift of silence and the opportunity to deepen her connection to herself and the world around her.

c) David gathers with his loved ones for a quiet celebration dinner at home to mark the conclusion of his 30-day journey. They share stories, reflections, and moments of gratitude for their shared experiences and the growth they've witnessed in each other throughout the past month. David expresses his appreciation for his friends and family's support and encouragement, acknowledging their role in his journey of self-discovery and personal transformation. Together, they appreciate the power of silence and its endless possibilities for renewal, growth, and connection.

www.ingramcontent.com/pod-product-compliance
Lightning Source LLC
Chambersburg PA
CBHW030450010526
44118CB00011B/866